Scarcity

SCARCITY

A Critique of the American Economy

Gus Tyler

Quadrangle/The New York Times Book Co.

Design by Ardashes Hamparian

Library of Congress Cataloging in Publication Data

Tyler, Gus.
    Scarcity: a critique of the American economy.

    Includes bibliographical references and index.
    1. United States—Economic conditions—1961–
I. Title.
HC106.6.T96   1976   330.9′73′092   75–36249
ISBN 0–8129–0611–X

Contents

Preface: The Argument

While the threat of scarcity arising from the exhaustion of Mother Earth is real, the present threat of scarcity in America is man-made. The maker of scarcity is an economic system dominated by the corporate conglomerate. To prepare plenty for the future, the nation must use its political power to subordinate these business megapowers to the public will by breaking up some, regulating others, and placing still others under public ownership. That is the thesis of this book.

The last quarter of the twentieth century is likely to be a terrible trauma for the American people. Scarcity will be doubly scary because it comes against the backdrop of assumed abundance. From the days of exploration to the present, America has been the land of promise, of potential plenty (Chapter I: The Assumption of Abundance).

The first great challenge to that assumption came in the 1930's with the Great Depression. Ultimately, the nation came out of that menacing malady to resume its trek toward affluence. But the recovery did not come easily because our policy-makers then—as today—were enmeshed in myths (Chapter 2: The Myth of Laissez Faire).

The chief myth was the divine powers of laissez faire: If the "people"—that is, the government—kept their hands off the economy, then there would be nothing to worry about in the long run. If scarcity did come in the form of a "crisis," then plenty would soon follow in the form of recovery. That's the way God had ordained it, and for politics to interfere with economics was a form of profanity.

After much suffering, however, America turned to the logical remedy: societal action to reform the economy. This mild form of socialism served the purpose from FDR to Lyndon Johnson (Chapter 3: The Return of Abundance).

In this age of apparent affluence, which concealed a continuing "scarcity" of the world's goods among large sectors of the population (Chapter 4: The Iron Law of Maldistribution), the corporations of America underwent profound transformations—in size and in character. The economy moved toward monopoly; monopolies merged into conglomerates; conglomerates became multinationals; financial corporations dominated the scene by moving in on industrial and agricultural production and distribution. What some earlier Marxist theoreticians once called "finance capitalism" became a fact of life in America (Chapters 5, 6, and 7: The Monopoly Game: Agribusiness; Scarcity in the City).

In this noncompetitive economy, it was no longer necessary for capitalists to produce more for less to lure customers. With concentrated control, the business elite could promote demand and limit supply to produce artificial scarcity—to charge more for less.

Until the 1970's, little attention was paid to this new kind of capitalism. To deal with the nation's economic problems, it was thought to be sufficient to play around with fiscal and monetary levers, while leaving the rest to the free play of supply and demand.

More recently, however, it has been necessary to take another hard look at the structure of the economy to explain the totally unexpected phenomenon called stagflation (Chapters 8, 9, and 10: Stagflation; Dependent America [Energy]; and Dependent America [Manufacture]). Those who insist upon remaining stuck in the old classical rut saw "stagflation" as a freak, a one-time crazy happening. But those who looked with a fresh eye at the simultaneous plague of unemployment and inflation concluded that the "unnatural" occurrence was no aberration but an inevitable expression of monopoly capitalism.

The chief response to the evils flowing from mounting corporate control of the society has been a shrill, highly moralistic cry for "corporate responsibility." Well-intentioned as this exhortation has been, it is an almost meaningless plea to *personae fictae* without a definable body or spirit, *sociétés anonymes* acting out the compulsions of their business beings (Chapter 11: Corporate Responsibility).

In other times, one might have expected the resurgence of a powerful socialist movement in the United States. The Marxist forecast of a small class in antisocial control of the means of production has come to pass. Surely the prophet should be honored by a great outpouring of the people on behalf of his ideas.

The responses to the present crises and dilemmas, however, have not been that simple—largely because the experiences of the world with "socialism" since the end of the First World War have moderated and modified the socialist answer (Chapter 12: Toward Abundance).

Just as the 1930's were a turning point in the relationship between politics and economics, eventuating in the New Deal, so in the 1970's there is likely to be another turning point to carry America beyond the New Deal. This book offers alternatives as we seek new directions for a future age of abundance.

Scarcity

I

The Assumption of Abundance

The American assumption has always been a New World of inexhaustible abundance. This premise is no longer true. To adjust to the finite reality will require radical changes in the economy, our political behavior and our values.

The assumption of abundance has been with us from the beginning. Columbus, Cortez, Cabot, and Hudson were outfitted by regal investors because the explorers and conquerors were expected to bring back riches: spices, furs, but mainly gold and silver. The Western Hemisphere was to provide the primitive accumulations that a nascent capitalism needed to grow into a world-encircling economy.

The settlers who followed put foot on a continent of boundless land. Here they found free soil, a heaven-ordained site for their various new Zions. And when the old Zion became a spiritual desert to some, they moved on to Rhode Island, to Ripon, to Salt Lake, to the open lands later inhabited by the Amish, the Mennonites, and the Cajuns to plant the seeds of a better Zion. America was a place of abundance for the spirit as well as the body.

At first the abundance was found on the Atlantic slope, the narrow strip that was an extension of Europe across the big water. When the land east of the Appalachians grew crowded—as in the old country—Americans moved westward by foot, by river, by covered wagon. And always there was more land, water, fish, fowl, and timber. And there were coal, iron and copper ore, oil, silver, and even that fabled gold.

The obstacles to abundance were transient challenges to stir the blood and whet the appetite. Indians to be cowed or killed. Deserts and mountains to be crossed. Distances to be spanned by the iron horse. Forests to be felled. Every stone in the way became a stepping-stone to new heights.

The riches of the land were multiplied by the richness of inventive minds. America became the land of better mousetraps, bulging factories, bigger buildings, autos, automats, and automation. Good meant bigger and better.

Whether the final product was always better is in doubt. But no doubt it was always bigger. And that was good, because size alone served our needs.

From the first, we looked for bigness, first in land and then in labor. We were short of skilled—even semiskilled—workers. The Jamestown Colony had proved the point lugubriously. The lords and ladies who had come to tidewater Virginia to enjoy the ease of this lush land suddenly found themselves in the cold claws of winter. They had not prepared for the bitter season: no real farmers, masons, carpenters, smiths to do the dirty work needed to survive. In its moment of desperation, the leisure class turned to cannibalism—literally.

The new land needed labor. But where was it to be found? The natural labor source should have been the Indians. But in North America—unlike in the Southern Hemisphere— the native tribes were predominantly nomadic. To enslave these stiff-necked spirits and to drill them in alien skills proved impossible. The settlers were satisfied to strip the savage of his lands and to chase him to some distant reservation.

In search of a bigger labor supply, the colonies turned to Africa. Yankee traders and Southern planters combined their talents to make early America the great slave nation of the Western civilization.

The North, whose terrain and trades were not congenial to slave labor, turned to Europe for indentured servants.

These short-term slaves were drawn from the human flotsam of the Old World. "If we leave out of account the substantial Puritan migration of 1630–40, not less than half, and perhaps considerably more of all the white immigrants to the colonies were indentured servants, redemptioners, or convicts."[1] After their years in service, these unfree toilers were liberated. But few had the skills to become respected craftsmen.

The free white artisan was in short supply—and he made the most of it. He was able to command double the wages of his European counterpart. By the time of the American Revolution, there were unions of the skilled: cordwainers, printers, ladies' tailors.

High wages became a prime stimulant of economic growth. First, the wages of workers became a significant factor in an expanding domestic market. Such mass consumption laid the basis for mass production. Second, higher wages meant higher production costs, goading producers into inventing or applying labor-saving devices. Together, high wages spurred mass production and improved productivity. This was true of colonial days and it remained true throughout the nation's history.

The Declaration of Independence and the Constitution of the United States laid the political foundations for economic growth. The Revolution cut the umbilical cord to the mother country; the colonies could now develop their own economies, free of British interference. The Constitution wiped out interstate tariff barriers, giving the makers of wares a "national" rather than just a local market.

The War of 1812—and the embargoes associated with it—strengthened America's resolve to become a strong and self-contained industrial society. Painfully aware that the young nation could not depend on foreign trade for survival, Anti-Federalist President Madison adapted and adopted the politico-economic principles of Federalist Hamilton: a national currency, a national bank, a protective tariff, and

[1] Richard Hofstadter, *America at 1750* (New York: Alfred A. Knopf, Inc., 1971), p. 34.

internal improvements, like turnpikes and canals, to "bind more closely together the various parts of our extended confederacy" into an independent economic entity.

This program of state aid to business—a commitment that has proliferated over the centuries—became known as the American System: a political plan for autonomous abundance. Said Henry Clay: "Dame Commerce is a flirting, flippant, noisy Jade and if we are governed by her fantasies, we shall never put off the muslins of India and the cloths of Europe." And so, quite deliberately, the first Republicans used the federal government to encourage American manufacture to give us our own muslins, cloth, furniture, and firearms.

An unplanned, unwanted, yet inevitable outgrowth of the American System was the growth of cities. Manufacture, trade, and finance brought people together in urban clusters for needed hands and heads. After 1820, cities sprouted: in the previous decade, only two cities of 8,000 inhabitants were added to the eleven already in existence; in the decade after, the number of such "large" cities doubled. Nationally, the urban population rose from less than 5 to almost 9 percent between 1820 and 1840.

Urbanization in America led—at an unusually early time —to political movements that, in turn, furthered the nation's capacity for economic growth. Out of the cities of the late 1820's came the Workingmen's Parties—first in Philadelphia and later in sixty more cities, mainly in New York, New Jersey, Vermont, Pennsylvania, Delaware, Ohio, and Connecticut. They were the first parties of laboring people in the world, the unique product of a nation that by the 1820's had extended the suffrage to men without property. While such a democratization of the ballot was a natural consequence of the egalitarian spirit of the American Revolution, the formation of "workies' parties" reveals much about the self-image of those who lived by the sweat of their brow. They were a prideful tribe, seriously bent on "equality."

These Workingmen's Parties were responsible for much of the agitation and organization leading to a system of free universal public education in the United States. While the education proposal was but one plank in labor's platform, it was the most universal, and—in the light of our nation's economic and political future—the most enduring and far-reaching. To the workies, free education meant that their children would be free to move up and out in a mobile society: better earners and better citizens, able to rise in the economic and political worlds. To the economy, education of the toiling classes meant a more intelligent (skilled) labor force. For the future of industry, this widespread schooling meant a great reservoir of learned people—scientists, inventors, technicians, managers—to turn their tutored talents to add to our abundance.

Although more and more people crowded into cities, more and more people spread across the land. The young were advised to go West. And when the old West began to run out, we got a new West. In 1846, we waged a war to take half of Mexico from Mexico, to annex the abundant area for a future Texas, Arizona, New Mexico, and California.

The annexation, however, gave us more than soil. It gave us the hard precious metals needed for commerce and finance. The Almighty himself seemed to have enlisted in the cause of a conquering capitalism when silver and gold were found in the peaks and valleys of the Rockies, awaiting the hand of the prospector. In 1845, an exuberant Democratic scribe goaded his countrymen on toward "the fulfillment of our manifest destiny to overspread the continent allotted by Providence for the free development of our yearly multiplying millions."

Abundance became contagious, creating a culture with its drives and demands to add to the abundance. Men made their riches to reinvest in the making of new riches. At least that's the way it was in the North, where a Puritan ethic of personal abstinence encouraged savings to spur an already galloping economy.

The aggressive capitalism of this dynamic North clashed with the classic agrarianism of the static South. In Dixie, the regnant slavocracy spent its income on the elegant life of manors, manners, and the manly arts of sport and war and statecraft. To make money just to have the money to make money seemed ungentlemanly—the mark of the bourgeois boor.

For a while, after the Revolution, it appeared that the South might change its ways and turn to manufacture. Southern planters who were hurt by the war were trying to recoup their fortunes with a good cash crop. They turned to cotton only to discover that it could not be raised and sold at a profitable price. A slave could spend a whole day separating cotton fluff from the seed only to clean one pound that sold at the exorbitant price of about thirty-five cents. But, with the invention of the cotton gin, Cotton became King. The South rediscovered the virtues of slavery. An illegal slave trade mushroomed poisonously. Slave population rose from under a million in 1800 to nearly four million by 1860. Slavery—the "peculiar institution" of the South—became a hallowed culture.

The clash of cultures—with attendant conflict over national economic policies and federal political power—led to the War between the States. The North—that is, the Union —won. While Abolitionists might see in this victory the avenging sword of the Almighty striking the chains of slavery, an historian with a realistic regard for martial might would more likely credit the victory of the North to its big population and its booming industry. Once more, it was abundance *über alles*.

Out of the Civil War issued a triple revolution: the North took top power from the South; the Negro was liberated from the plantation; the American peasantry won title to its own land. All three revolutions added to our abundance.

In the prewar years, the White House was primarily a Southern residence—almost totally so at first. The Presidents of the Virginia Dynasty—Washington, Jefferson, Madison, and Monroe—served two terms each, interrupted by a one-term John Adams from Massachusetts. After a second Adams (John Q.), came Jackson, a Tennessean who was born in Waxhaw, South Carolina. His Vice-President, Martin Van Buren, was the first Northerner ever elected to the presidency outside the Adams family. He was succeeded by William Henry Harrison, a Hoosier who was born in

Charles City County Virginia. His early death made way for his Vice-President John Tyler of Virginia. The next two Presidents were Polk of North Carolina and Taylor, whose residence was Kentucky, but whose birthplace was Orange County, Virginia. Only after that administration did the North begin to move in on the White House with Fillmore, Pierce, Buchanan, and Lincoln. In the one hundred years after the Civil War, however (from Abraham Lincoln in 1864 to Lyndon Baines Johnson in 1964), no Southerner was elected to the presidency.

The transfer of power in Washington from South to North transformed the country. The federal authority was used to grant rights of way to railway corporations. An iron web tied markets, materials, and manufacturers into a tighter economic unit. Rich mineral lands were leased, sold, and given away to economically ambitious and politically shrewd operators. The capitalist dynamic became the national dynamo—to exploit and to expand without end.

The liberation of the Negro opened up a supply of cheap labor for the North. The flow from plantation to plant was very slow in the first years when liberation simply meant— for most Negroes—the freedom to starve. No master, no job, no portable skill, no home, no anything. But in time, the trickle North became a stream and later a flood from southern farms to northern cities. This huge migration gave industry the hands it needed to add to our abundance.

The Homestead Act (1862), granting 160 acres to any settler who would work the land for five years, encouraged a movement into new territories. Forests were felled, lands cleared, farms founded to turn territories into states, dotted with new towns and then cities. The Homestead Act was America's bloodless peasant revolution. It became a political basis for the family farm that would one day make the United States the foodbasket of the world.

As new farms and factories flourished, they drew their hands not only from the old cities of the North and the old plantations of the South, but from everywhere. The railroads were built by the Chinese, Irish, and Mexicans. The soil of the old Northwest and the new Midwest was tilled by

Scandinavians and Germans. The bowels of the earth were dug up by Italians, Slavs, Welsh. The world beat a path to America's door to enter the land of abundance. Two and a half million immigrants arrived from Europe in the 1870's; in the next decade, the number doubled.

Industry grew apace. From 1859 to 1899, the value of manufactured products rose from $1.8 billion to $13 billion. America was now turning out more than England or Germany.

Europe sent its capital as well as its manpower to add to our abundance. In one year (1871), London bought up $110 million in American securities. Before the turn of the century, foreign investors had poured more than $4 billion into the United States.

To the prescient, at the turn of the century, it should have been clear that abundance was not only an American assumption but an American actuality. To the sensitive, however, it should also have been apparent that this abundance was accumulating in ways that would ultimately imperil both the material and social fabric of the nation.

Crusading capital tore across the land, ravishing and ruining irreplaceable resources. Forests were felled for lumber, leaving nothing behind but the sad stumps of once-proud trees. Without live growth to hold the soil, the rains ran wild to flood fields and towns. Animal's hooves beat once-fertile soil into hardpan and then into dust bowls. The beautiful green hills of the Appalachians were scarred and bled for their coal. Industrial waste polluted fresh waters; smokestacks poisoned clean air; indigestible waste choked the land.

The assumption, of course, was that the country was too big and too ever-giving to be exhausted. Hence, it was not until the twentieth century that the idea of conservation gained any currency. And then, only in a rather wan way— like replacing trees that had been chopped down.

Crusading capital also identified national abundance with its own abundance. So long as the rich were getting richer, all would be well with the nation—for then the rich would have the means to invest to become even richer, ad infinitum. And since no individual had the necessary riches to build and run the railroads, to buy and operate the mines, to generate and distribute electricity, to extract and merchandise oil, a fictional person was created, known as the corporation.

By the turn of the century, it was apparent to social critics that these corporations were not, in the first place, set up to provide abundance to all, but to provide superabundance to their owners. Voices now began to cry out against the poverty amidst plenty, the scarcity amidst superfluity. Reformers feared not only economic despotism imposed by such corporations on the worker and consumer and small businessman but also a political tyranny as wealth bought the governmental influences over the commonwealth.

"The power of groups of men organized by incorporation as joint-stock companies, or of small knots of rich men acting in combination, has developed with unexpected strength in unexpected ways, overshadowing individuals and even communities, and showing that the very freedom of association which men sought to secure by law . . . may, under the shelter of the law, ripen into a new form of tyranny," wrote James Bryce in *The American Commonwealth*.

"The decade of the nineties," records historian Henry Commager, "is the watershed of American history. . . . In this period came at last a full-throated recognition of the crowding problems of agriculture, urban life, slums, trusts, business and political corruption, race prejudice and the maldistribution of wealth."

The instinctive response of those who rejected the new tyranny and its attendant evils was to turn from the ugly present to the beautiful past. If the trusts were to blame, then the thing to do was to bust the trusts: the socialism of the petite bourgeoisie.

The official house of labor—the once-dominant Noble and Holy Order of the Knights of Labor—endorsed the idea of a return to small business. Although the Knights did strike and bargain and sign contracts, they viewed all such activity as of secondary worth. Their real interest was in cheap money and low credit to enable workers to own their own tools or to set up worker cooperatives to produce products for sale.

The movement against the corporations crystallized in the Sherman Anti-Trust Act that made every conspiracy or combination in restraint of trade or commerce a crime. The act was intended to defend old-fashioned against new-fashioned capitalism.

Despite an occasional foray by the federal government against some trust, here and there, now and then, the great combines continued to combine. And they have never stopped.

To produce in abundance requires a productive machinery that can operate with the economies of bigness. That requires great capital outlay. To take advantage of sophisticated techniques—to research, develop, and apply—requires heavy capitalization. To undertake such investments in a risky market that can be taken away by competitors would be impossible for prudent investors. Hence, great combines —corporations, oligopolies, cartels, and monopolies—are established to raise the needed capital and to minimize the risks of an uncontrolled market.

The inexorable logic for bigness made the antitrust act an anachronism at the height of its popularity. Political considerations, too, helped make the law a dead letter. The Sherman Anti-Trust Act (1890) was passed by a federal legislature "more interested in quieting the public clamor for action against the trusts than in actually breaking up any of the new combinations."[2] The Chief Executives in charge of enforcing the law, including trustbuster Theodore Roosevelt himself, had no intention of breaking up the big combines. "Much of the legislation enacted against the trusts," declared TR in 1900, "is not one whit more intelligent than the mediaeval bull against the comet, and has not been one article more effective." He insisted that to put an end to the age of industrial giants would "turn back the wheels of modern progress." Finally, TR gave his bully endorsement to the notion that making the rich richer means

2 John A. Garraty, *The American Nation* (New York: Harper & Row, 1966), p. 521.

making everyone richer. "In our industrial and social system, the interests of all men are so closely intertwined that in the immense majority of cases a straight-dealing man who by his efficiency, by his ingenuity and industry, benefits himself must also benefit others."

Roosevelt favored regulation, rather than abolition, of the giants. But regulation was bound to be of little use for reasons classically stated by Richard Olney, President Cleveland's Attorney General, in a letter to a railroad president who wanted to wipe out the "regulatory" Interstate Commerce Commission: "The Commission as its functions have now been limited by the courts, is, or can be made, of great use to the railroads. It satisfies the popular clamor for a government supervision of railroads, at the same time that such supervision is almost entirely nominal. Further, the older such a commission gets to be, the more inclined it will be found to take the business and railroad view of things. It thus becomes a sort of barrier between the railroad corporations and the people and a sort of protection against hasty and crude legislation hostile to railroad interests. The part of wisdom is not to destroy the Commission, but to utilize it."

By 1911, in the Standard Oil Case, the Supreme Court also joined in the nullification—at least, the castration— of the antitrust act, when Chief Justice White promulgated the Rule of Reason. Only those combines should be tamed that were engaged in "unreasonable" restraints of trade. And who should decide what was "unreasonable"? The Executive and the Judiciary filled with men who owed their high posts to high finance.

The tragic demise of the antitrust act became a tragi-comedy when in 1912 the Supreme Court turned the Sherman Anti Trust Act against the hatters' union, assessing them for triple damages in a strike against a shop in Danbury, Connecticut.

Whatever the outcries against corporations, the corporate way continued to flourish. By and large, people accepted the idea of big business—because bigger meant better, getting more for less. As Andrew Carnegie put it bluntly:

the oppression of mass manufacture was the price paid for luxury.

"Formerly articles were manufactured at the domestic hearth, or in small shops which formed part of the household. The master and his apprentices worked side by side, the latter living with the master, and therefore subject to the same conditions. . . . There was, substantially, social equality and even political equality. . . . The inevitable result of such a mode of manufacture was crude articles at high prices. Today the world obtains commodities of excellent quality at prices which even the preceding generation would have deemed incredible. . . . The poor enjoy what the rich could not before afford."[3]

The growth of corporations and of the economy was spurred by two wars—the Spanish-American and World War I.

The United States had long looked upon Cuba as a desirable possession: John Quincy Adams would gladly have annexed the island if he had not feared it would be still another slave state. Said Thomas Jefferson of then Spanish-held New Orleans: "There is on the globe one single spot, the possessor of which is our natural enemy. It is New Orleans." When Spain transferred the Mississippi basin to Napoleon, Jefferson put on all possible pressure for the Louisiana Purchase. In 1819, the United States "purchased" Florida from Spain by handing over $5 million to Americans who had claims against Spain. The acquisition of the Southwest from Mexico was a continuation of the same clash between an expanding America and a declining Spanish power. By 1896, America was ready to move to liberate Cuba from Spanish tyranny. In the process, we picked up the Philippines. It was obviously our manifest destiny to be a world power. "The United States," commented a French diplomat, "is seated at the table where the great game is played, and it can not leave it." We were doomed to greatness.

World War I reinforced our sense of seeming destiny—

[3] Andrew Carnegie, *The Gospel of Wealth* (Cambridge: Harvard University Press, 1962), p. 15–16.

both economically and politically. With several million men in uniform, the nation still had to produce enough to meet civilian as well as military needs. To step up productivity, manufacture turned to "rationalization" of production—a forerunner of automation. Manufacture itself became more important—as contrasted with transportation and extraction—as factories sprung into being to build cars, tanks, planes, guns. America issued from the war as the world's top maker of things.

Politically, the United States became a central—if not the central—world power. Our entrance into the war gave the victory to the Allies. In negotiating the postwar settlement, American President Woodrow Wilson's was the decisive voice.

To Americans of the 1920's, none of this was a surprise. We were doing what came naturally—fulfilling our destiny as the biggest and the best, without end.

"We in America today are nearer to the final triumph over poverty than ever before in the history of any land," proclaimed Herbert Hoover as the Republican candidate for President in 1928. "The poorhouse is vanishing from among us. We have not yet reached the goal, but given a chance to go forward with the policies of the last eight years, we shall soon with the help of God be in sight of the day when poverty will be banished from the nation."

With this appeal, Hoover won the election with 444 electoral votes to his Democratic opponent's 87. On Inauguration Day, 1929, the newly elected President of the United States announced flatly: "We have reached a higher degree of comfort and security than ever existed before in the history of the world."

But in October of that year, the American dream of abundance-for-all turned into a nightmare. On the twenty-fourth of the month—Black Thursday—stocks slipped disastrously. Bankers met in a hurried noontime session to vow multi-million-dollar pledges to support the market. The President hastened to calm the nation's nerves by announcing that "the fundamental business of the country, that is production and distribution of commodities, is on a sound and prosperous basis." But it was all to no avail. The following Tuesday, the market plunged into a bottomless abyss.

For salvation, the President turned to faith, hope, and charity. He had faith that if the businessmen of the country showed goodwill, the economy would revive. So Hoover made repeated appeals to management to maintain jobs and wage levels.

He sought to inspire hope. In March 1930, he spoke optimistically about an end to the depression in a short matter of sixty days. Two months later, he pepped up the Chamber of Commerce with his conviction "that we have now passed the worst and with continued unity of effort we shall rapidly recover." Others joined the hope chorus. Thus, Henry Ford on November 14: "Any lack of confidence in the economic future of the basic strength of business in the United States is foolish." Charles Schwab, Chairman of the Board of Bethlehem Steel on December 10: "Never before has American business been as firmly entrenched for prosperity as it is today." Cincinnati tried to beat the blues by distributing lapel buttons reading: "I'm sold on America. I won't talk depression." The crisis was treated as a psychosomatic ailment that could be treated with verbal therapy.

Hoover looked to charity to ease the suffering of the unfortunate victims of the devastating unemployment. He called for "block aid," for the more affluent on the street to salvage their hungry brethren.

To the best official brains of the time, the unsettling stock-market crash was just a jolt on the highroad to ever-expanding plenty. There had been such crises before—recognized as unfortunately bothersome episodes in the recurrent business cycles. To distinguish between such "crises" and the letdown in 1929, the official phrasemakers of the day decided to call the setback a mere "depression," a sort of minor dent on the smooth surface of our "sound and prosperous" society.

Since all was well—or would shortly be well—with the old-fashioned way of doing things, Hoover resisted any newfangled capers by the federal government. While he had no objection to aid for the needy coming from private charity or state governments, he was opposed to using federal funds either to spur public works or to provide direct relief. Hoover knew his priorities: "The primary duty of government," he asserted, was "to hold expenditures within our income." He did not believe that "prosperity" could be "restored by raids upon the Public treasury." He made it clear that he was "opposed to any direct or indirect government dole" to the jobless. He vetoed Senator Norris's proposal to provide work to the unemployed through a Tennessee Valley project, because, Hoover reiterated, "I am firmly opposed to the Government entering any business the major purpose of which is competition with our citizens."

Basically, Hoover's medicine was to let the malady remedy itself. If things got bad enough they would then get better. Andrew Mellon—Secretary of the Treasury under three Republican Presidents—sloganized the prescription: "Liquidate labor, liquidate stock, liquidate the farmers." Once all was liquid, the waters of the frozen economy would flow again.

In the opening years of the 1930's, this liquidation became a reality. Labor was being liquidated as unemployment rose to four million in 1930, to seven million in 1931, and to eleven million in 1932. Those who somehow found jobs earned less: total labor income fell from $54 billion in 1929 to $31.5 billion in 1932. Average salaries fell 40 percent, and manufacturing wages, 60 percent. Stocks were being liquidated. Between 1929 and 1932, new capital issues fell from $10 billion to $1 billion. In the same four years, more than 100,000 businesses went bankrupt and banks perished by the hundreds and then thousands every year. Farmers were being liquidated. Rather than sell corn for close to nothing, farmers burned the food for fuel—while millions went hungry. Farms were foreclosed. The spokesmen for the Wisconsin Farmers' Union told Congress that some of his members would like to "come down here to Washington to blow you fellows all up."

The ancient assumption of abundance seemed to have gone with the crash. The economy collapsed under the burden of plenitude. We had overproduced. America became a complex of contradictions. Riches had brought on poverty. Plenty had caused a scarcity—of jobs, income, homes, clothes, food, and even hope. Our historic strength, the power to create, became our near fatal weakness.

Our failure had come from our success in building a productive machine that was turning out more than we were consuming. Marriner S. Eccles, chairman of the Board of Governors of the Federal Reserve System, explained our embarrassment of riches: "We sustained a high level of employment . . . with the aid of an exceptional expansion of debt outside of the banking system. This debt was provided by a large growth of business savings as well as by savings of individuals, particularly in the upper-income groups where taxes were . . . low. . . . Had there been a better distribution of the current income from the national product—in other words, had there been less savings by business and the higher-income groups and more income in the lower groups—we should have had far greater stability in our economy. Had the six billion dollars, for instance, that were loaned by corporations and wealthy individuals for stock market speculations been distributed to the public as lower prices or higher wages and with less profits to the corporations and the well-to-do, it would have prevented or greatly moderated the economic collapse that began at the end of 1929."[4]

Our assumption had been that if capitalism had enough capital to invest, all would be well. Now we discovered that the capitalists had overinvested: they did not lack the means to produce but they did lack the customers to buy. As the rising number of agitators at the time raged: we were not suffering from overproduction but from underconsumption.

Yet, ironically, the central theme of Hoover's recovery

[4] Marriner S. Eccles, *Beckoning Frontiers: Public and Personal Recollections* 1951. Cited by John M. Blum et al., *The National Experience* (New York: Harcourt, Brace and World, 1968), p. 661.

program was to make the rich richer—especially the financial institutions. In 1932, he set up the Reconstruction Finance Corporation to make Treasury funds available as loans to businesses. Not all business: just banks, insurance companies, and railroads. As applied in practice, about half the sum dispensed went to three large banks, one of which was headed by Charles G. Dawes, who was also head of the RFC but who had the good grace to resign his public post shortly before the loan to his own bank was approved. A similar piece of legislation—the Glass-Steagall Act—liberalized the lending power of banks by making government bonds acceptable as collateral for Federal Reserve notes. This meant more power to the banks. A further measure— the Federal Home Loan Bank—gave financial assistance to savings banks, insurance companies, and building-and-loan associations.

In the Hooverian cosmology, these funds that flowed from the people's treasury to the financial institutions to the corporations were envisioned as flowing back to the people. In the words of the folksy Will Rogers, "the money was all appropriated for the top in the hopes that it would trickle down to the needy."

To the needy, however, this was all a plot to soak the poor to enrich the rich. In the words of the embittered bonus marchers who descended on the nation's capital to demand recognition for their past services and their present plight:

> *Mellon pulled the whistle,*
> *Hoover rang the bell,*
> *Wall Street gave the signal*
> *and the country went to hell.*

The milk of abundance had soured into scarcity. And scarcity became the new religion. "When a terrible drought struck the country in 1930, many farmers rejoiced, and stock prices soared on Wall Street. The Federal Farm Board urged southern planters to plow under every third row of cotton, and even the boll weevil was viewed with a friendlier eye. Brazil burned thousands of bags of coffee and shoveled scowloads of coffee into the Atlantic. Rubber planters were jubilant when they discovered a new pest was attacking their trees."[5] Suddenly, abundance had become bad and scarcity became the great new good.

[5] William Leuchtenberg, *The Perils of Prosperity* (Chicago: University of Chicago Press, 1951), p. 260.

The Myth of Laissez Faire

According to the mythology of American capitalism, the economy ran itself without help or hindrance from the state up until the time of the New Deal. Economists referred to this separation of economics from politics as laissez faire. Politicians translated this French phrase into the very American slogan of "rugged individualism."

This nonsystem was hailed by learned men as heaven-ordained. "Things regulate themselves," proclaimed Harvard's Francis Bowen, "which means, of course, that God regulates them by his general laws, which always, in the long run, work to good." For man to enact his own laws over the natural economic laws was both stupid and sacrilegious. Such evil deeds were also un-American, a threat to a free economy.

For several generations, laissez faire was the regnant doctrine in economic thought, political rhetoric, and Supreme Court opinions. So profound was its influence that even today there are well-placed devotees of the allegedly traditional way who demand that the "invisible hand" of the economic Almighty be liberated from the fetters of an oppressive welfare state.

Yet, this image of a "free enterprise" system is pure myth. The record reveals that business repeatedly used government to make and multiply riches. Indeed, the story of the great American fortunes is largely the chronicle of entrepreneurs using political contacts and controls to accumulate economic wealth that, in turn, was used to strengthen political influence for greater pecuniary gain.

To set the record straight is not just to debunk a myth but also to reveal how a fable has been used one-sidedly to favor private gain over public good, ultimately to turn abundance into scarcity. It is also to suggest that the state has historically been an instrument of economic action that can be used in the future to turn scarcity into abundance.

The discovery and exploration of the New World were political acts. The Spanish government subsidized Columbus; England's Henry VII backed John Cabot; France supported Giovanni Verrazzano; Holland dispatched Henry Hudson. All these voyages were economic ventures launched by governments, sponsored by states in search of riches.

Settlement of the new continent was equally political, initiated by state decrees that granted huge tracts of lands to companies or to persons who were favored by the Crown. The vast expanse from Maine to Cape Fear was granted by James I to two companies: the Virginia Company of London for the southern portion and the Virginia Company of Plymouth for the northern. The companies were run by men of means who, from the outset, turned the collective effort into personal profit.

In this, they were aided by the British government. Since the companies alleged that it was their highest purpose to Christianize the heathen Indian, the ventures were treated as "pious" orders and granted the right to raise funds by lottery. The companies were also treated to cheap labor, in line with their objective of helping the mother country to unload "the unprofitable increase in our people," the "superfluous twigs" who had been cut loose from the soil by enclosure. These hapless hungry were sold into indentured servitude.

Although the colony boasted that "our principal wealth consists of servants," there still were not enough of them. So the Crown chartered the Royal African Company to capture and deliver black slaves.

Since the original Virginia was far too large to handle centrally, the Crown subdivided the area by making huge grants to people with the right political pull. Under these "proprietaries," the owner was both political and economic boss. Maryland was founded as a gift from Charles I to the prominent Catholic Lord Baltimore; Carolina was established as a feudal state by eight members of the Stuart retinue.

The motives of these users of state power were put plainly by the Secretary to the Lords Proprietors of Carolina, when he asked himself: "What commodities shall I be able to produce that will yield me money in other countries that I may be enabled to buy Negro Slaves."

Instinctively aware of the economic worth of political power, these colonial proprietors made it clear that they had no intention of sharing their rule with any but their own kind. The Carolina constitution stipulated that "all power and dominion is most naturally founded on property" and that it was necessary to avoid "erecting a numerous democracy." New England's John Cotton thundered: "Democracy God did [not] ordain as a fit government either for church or commonwealth. If the people be governors, who shall be governed?"

The great middle colony of New York (New Netherlands) was settled by the Dutch West Indies Company under generous grants from the States General of Holland. Vast tracts were parceled out to "patroons," who by settling fifty "souls" on their land won title to the property forever. Profits were drawn not only from the soil but from the timber of dense forests and from the rivers and bays and oceans teeming with fish. The patroon named public officials, policed his bailiwicks, wrote the law "according to his will and pleasure"—a prerogative he could pass on to his heirs and assigns.

When the British conquered New York, they continued to use political power for economic gain—in their own fashion. One of the most notorious converters of public office into personal profit was the royal appointee Governor

Fletcher. He gave away land in exchange for bribes. To Captain John R. N. Evans he granted a Hudson Valley tract that ran forty miles one way and thirty miles another for the paltry bribe of one hundred pounds. Nicholas Bayard got an estate of equal size around Schoharie Creek. Bayard served Fletcher as a "fixer" and "bag-man" who handled the payoffs from sea pirates seeking to buy immunity from the governor. Later, when Fletcher was transferred to Pennsylvania to serve as Governor of the Commonwealth, he carried his practices with him.

The political power that was used to grab the lands was also used to hold the lands. When the Earl of Bellomont— who had been appointed Governor of Massachusetts Bay, New York, and other provinces—wished to move against the great landgrabbers by confiscating their estates, he turned to the British Parliament to perform the act, because he feared that he would "not have strength enough in the assembly of New York to break them."

Political power *within* the estate gave the proprietor added sources of income: "He forced his tenants to sign covenants that they should trade in nothing else than the produce of the manor; that they should trade nowhere else but at his store; that they should grind the flour at his mill, and buy bread at his bakery, lumber at his sawmills and liquor at his brewery. . . . These feudal tenures were established in law."[1]

In colonies such as Massachusetts, where there was no patroon system, the bothersome problem of wages was handled by legislation and decrees to hold down the laborer's earnings. When a depression hit Massachusetts in 1641, the General Court decided that wages had to be cut to keep business profitable. Since entrepreneurs could not be expected to "spend the small remainder of their estates for the maintenance of others in such a way as will not offer them some equal recompense," it was decreed that all workers and servants "lower their wages according to the fall in the price of commodities." In similar bills in 1670

[1] Gustavus Myers, *History of the Great American Fortunes* (New York: Modern Library, 1936), p. 51.

and 1672, farmers were protected against hands who were spending their wages for fancy dress "altogether unbecoming their place and rank." Employees who violated such laws had to make "double restitution to their employers and to pay a fine of double the excess value."[2] In Pennsylvania, county courts were empowered to set wages at "a just rate."

Monopolies in various undertakings were officially granted by colonies. While some, as in the case of Massachusetts, limited such grants to inventions for the public good, the definition was broad enough to include grist mills, bridges, transport, and the Indian fur trade. The attitude of businessmen toward official grants of monopoly was two-faced. Where a company held a natural monopoly it resisted state grant—and regulation; where a company needed official authority to establish a monopoly, it favored the state action.

An almost too perfect case of entrepreneurial attitude toward monopoly is that of William Pynchon, who by virtue of strategic location in Springfield and his talents as a manipulator had established an effective one-man control over the fur trade. When Connecticut officially granted him a monopoly that established the colony's right to regulate and tax as well, Pynchon protested to the heavens. It was, he declaimed, against "the public goode and the liberty of free men to make a monopoly of trade. . . . I hope the Lord in his mercy will keep me from coveting any unlawful gaines; or [agreeing to] any man's hindrance where God doth not hinder them."

To get the best price on its proudest product, Virginia wrote a law governing the sale of tobacco. All the crop was gathered in a storehouse. The poorest stuff—"trash tobacco" —was destroyed. The rest was put on the market. The artificial scarcity brought a high price for the tobacco available for sale.

The American Revolution was a major political act to liberate the American entrepreneur from British restrictions. In the North, a typical complaint ran, "A colonist can not make a button, horseshoe, nor a hob-nail, but some sooty

[2] Joseph Dorfman, *The Economic Mind in American Civilization* (New York: Viking Press, 1946), pp. 45–6.

ironmonger or respectable button-maker of Britain shall bawl and squeal that his honor's worship is most egregiously maltreated, injured, cheated and robbed by the rascally American republican." When British howls turned into legislation to restrict colonial trade and manufacture, there were "loud howls of protest from prosperous influential Yankees."[3] In the South, the great planters needed a revolution to liberate them from a mounting indebtedness to British merchants. Colonial staples were sold in London to merchants who set their prices almost unilaterally. Manufactured items were bought overseas at prices that were again set almost unilaterally by British merchants. To make ends meet, southern planters went into debt, pledging future crops to pay for current purchases. This impending impoverishment of wealthy plantation masters made them, in the words of one Virginia governor, "uneasy, peevish, and ready to murmur at every Occurrence." The Revolution was one such massive murmur—an act by thirteen small states to lay the foundation for an independent American economy.

In the post-Revolutionary years of the Articles of Confederation, North and South engaged in a political tug of war over whether or not Spain should allow free navigation of the Mississippi River. The North (actually the Northeast) said no. Its reason, according to then-Colonel James Monroe, was to "keep the weight of population eastward . . . to appreciate the vacant lands of Massachusetts and New York." Also, the Northeast did not want to see its labor supply drained westward. The South, on the other hand, favored Spain's opening the Mississippi because the movement of goods from the old Northwest to New Orleans would favor the South.

To tie a developing West more closely to the South, Washington and Madison proposed a canal that would bring backwood wares to the James and Potomac Rivers and thence to ocean ports. Virginia and Maryland passed the necessary bills to establish a development company, with each state purchasing ten percent of the shares.

[3] The Editors of American Heritage, *The Revolution* (New York: American Heritage Publishing Co., 1971), pp. 79–81.

At the Constitutional Convention, central colloquies revolved around economic questions. Property had to be protected against the envy of the propertyless. Madison was worried about that great multitude of those who, in the future, would "secretly sigh for a more equal distribution of life's blessings." Very much aware of Shay's Rebellion, he noted that "symptoms of a levelling spirit . . . have sufficiently appeared in a certain quarter to give notice of the future danger." The Constitution was designed to protect the haves from the assaults of the have-nots.

Should the slave trade be halted? Virginia and Maryland had forbidden it; Georgia and South Carolina had not. The latter argued that the former wanted to put an end to the importation of Africans in order to boost the price on slaves.

Should the central government have the power to regulate commerce? Yes and no, depending on what economic interest predominated in what state. The result was a compromise to empower Congress to establish regulations but not to impose duties on exports.

In the great debate on the ratification of the Constitution, the intimate relationship between political power and economic interest was laid bare. More than a half a century before Karl Marx was to enunciate his economic interpretation of history, James Madison spelled out the concept in Federalist Paper No. 10:

"The most common and durable source of factions has been the various and unequal distribution of property. Those who hold and those who are without property have ever formed distinct interests in society. Those who are creditors and those who are debtors fall under a like discrimination. A landed interest, a manufacturing interest, a mercantile interest, a money interest, with many lesser interests, grow up of necessity in civilized nations, and divide them into different classes, actuated by different sentiments and views. The regulation of these various and interfering interests forms the principal task of modern legislation, and involves the spirit of party and faction in the necessary and ordinary operations of the government."

Needless to say, the interests best equipped to take hold

of the political process and turn it to their own purposes were those who understood how public power could be used for private profit. Within a decade after the ratification of the Constitution, gentlemen of means got the government to provide them with public funds, monopolies, and special prerogatives to set up transport, manufacture, real-estate speculation, and banks.

In 1791, the Pennsylvania Society for Promoting the Improvement of Roads and Inland Navigation, headed by the ever-enterprising Robert Morris, asked for state aid to set up a system of roads and canals. While allowing that the state was to fix tolls, the state was also expected to make up the deficiency if revenues did not yield 6 percent on investment. Also the state had to stipulate that it would not charter any competitors for some time.

The Pennsylvania legislature agreed, setting up three such companies with the ubiquitous Robert Morris as president of all of them. To help swell their capital, the state granted the company the right to run a $400,000 lottery.

In Paterson, New Jersey, a charter for incorporation was granted to the New Jersey Society for Useful Manufactures. "The capital required would be supplied by using the public debt; the labor supply necessary for the labor-saving machinery would be composed of women and children and emigrants obtained 'on reasonable terms in countries where labor is cheap.' For proper policing of the inhabitants of the place, the principal seat of the factories was to be incorporated."[4]

The company was also granted the right to run a lottery and was given the power of eminent domain should it want to build a canal to facilitate its purposes. Its employes were also exempted from military service and from taxes.

In 1795, Georgia granted 35 million acres to four interlocked companies for half a million dollars. Just about everybody who was anybody in land speculation, including Supreme Court Justice James Wilson, was in on the deal. The whole arrangement was of doubtful legality, since Georgia was selling land that did not belong to it and since, as

[4] Dorfman, *Economic Mind*, p. 291.

Albert Gallatin put it, "the agents who pretended to sell the property of their constituents, were, with the exception of a single person, interested in and parties to the purchase."

When the Republicans—Jefferson—took over from the Federalists—Adams—there was a rash of new banks. "New charters were needed," it was argued, "for Republican banks in order to counteract the political influence of the Federalists, who controlled the existing banks."[5]

Because public opinion resented and political opposition resisted the chartering of new banks, a number of would-be bankers set themselves up as something else with a backdoor arrangement to go into banking. Thus the Kentucky Insurance Company of Lexington was set up as an "association of patriotic gentlemen" to insure boats on the Ohio and Mississippi Rivers. But a small-print clause allowed it to issue notes that were negotiable. Soon this insurance-company-turned-bank was showing dividends of 19 percent under the guidance of the most political Henry Clay, the company's attorney.

While states were encouraging "associations of patriotic gentlemen" to set up their companies with public funds and grants of monopoly, the same states were discouraging—indeed, outlawing—associations of ungentlemanly laborers who sought to set up unions. In the 1805 case of the Philadelphia Cordwainers (shoemakers), the prosecution argued that while a worker "might lawfully ask whatever he thought proper for himself, where two or more agreed to ask the same prices, they are guilty of a violation of the law." The unionists were found "guilty of a combination to raise wages" and were fined. This decision set a precedent for later trials against New York tailors (1809), Baltimore and Pittsburgh shoemakers (1814 and 1815). In regard to the last, the court recorder opined: "The verdict of the jury is most important to the manufacturing interests of the community for it puts an end to these associations which have been so prejudicial to the successful enterprise of the capitalist in the western country."

A labor leader, Stephen Simpson, retorted: "If mechanics

5 Ibid., p. 331.

combine to raise wages, the laws punish them as conspirators against the good of society, and the dungeon awaits them as it does the robber. But the laws have made it a just and meritorious act, that capitalists shall combine to strip the man of labour of his earnings, and reduce him to a dry crust, and a gourd of water. Thus does power invert justice."

In these "conspiracy trials" against the early unions, the courts had no legislation at all on which to base their decisions. So they arrogated the power to themselves under the ancient British theory of the common law: the judges legislated from the bench. For them it was axiomatic that one of the prime purposes of law was to help along the "successful enterprise of the capitalist."

While entrepreneurs looked to the Constitution and the courts to protect their property and to promote their purposes, they were quite ready to defy all law to the point of secession when they found federal policies to be contrary to their special interests. During the War of 1812, New England merchants and shippers who saw the conflict ruining their commercial operations were enthusiastic about the decision of their states to withdraw from the United States unless the war was halted. At the Hartford Convention, called to organize this secession, the articulate Daniel Webster explained the economic origins of the war: a plot by the South to ruin the commerce of the North in order to erect a southern despotism. Robert Goodloe Harper—a Republican turned Federalist—seconded the thesis: the war, like the American Revolution itself, was just a way for indebted southern planters to get rid of their British creditors. "The influence of such a state of things in fostering the spirit of resistance and the desire for separation (from England) cannot be doubted," he explained matter-of-factly, "unless we doubt the operation of self interest and passion on human conduct."

When, in 1832, Congress passed a tariff law that South Carolina considered prejudicial to its business interests—a "tariff of abominations"—the state called a Convention that pronounced the law as "unauthorized by the Constitution" and therefore "null, void and no law, nor binding upon this State, its officers or citizens." Should the federal government try to coerce the state, South Carolina would secede.

In 1832, this southern state stood alone. A generation later, it was joined by the other states of the Confederacy that seceded from the Union.

The Hartford Convention, the Act of Nullification, the Civil War were obviously all political, highly political, acts, undertaken at the instance of propertied men to perpetuate their economic way of life. In no case were the monied motives hidden. It was simply assumed that, the impact of "self interest on human conduct" being what it is, the business of politics must necessarily entail business.

The case of the "godlike Daniel Webster" suggests the openness of the tie between finance and legislation in an earlier era. In the great Compromise of 1850, there was a curious clause that gave $10 million to Texas for the loss of territory in a boundary settlement, which funds would go mainly to pay off bonds that had been issued by the Republic of Texas before it was annexed. Most of these bonds were held by the Washington banking firm of Corcoran and Riggs, whose principals were very popular around Capitol Hill, always ready to extend a helping hand to a congressman in need of a fast loan—including the awesome Daniel Webster, who owed the bank $10,000—no mean sum in those days. It was this same sixty-nine-year-old Webster who carried the day for the bill in a history-making oration of three hours and eleven minutes. The bank, in the person of William W. Corcoran, was so grateful to Webster that it returned his $10,000 note, marked "Cancelled, Paid in Full," and then added another $1,000 as a gratuity.

When the last of the compromises was exhausted, the impending conflict became the bloodiest war in the nation's history: North against South, abolitionist against slaveholder, unionist against secessionist. No doubt the causes of the war were many. But for the American capitalist, the War between the States was a political act, a revolution, that put the northern men of money in the decisive seats of power.

"Of all the nations that have industrialized their economies through capitalistic rather than socialistic methods, the United States offered its businessmen the greatest encouragement and the fewest obstacles. . . . The war . . . taught the government habits of openhanded and reckless generosity toward private enterprise that sought control of public funds and public resources."[6]

A foreign scholar-observer, M. I. Ostrogorski, summed up the relationship between the men who ran the government and the men who ran the economy: "From one end of the scale to the other, the constituted authorities are unequal to their duty. . . . [They] even place the power which has been entrusted to them by the community at the disposal of private interests."

The greatest wealth of the federal government was in land. And this land was given away by the tens of millions of acres to a handful of businessmen with the right political connections. Foremost among these were the railroaders.

Even before the Civil War "the railroad . . . was beginning to dominate not only transportation in the United States, but the whole of American life."[7] The roads opened new areas for exploitation, for markets, for living. The roads were the nation's circulatory system. They served America as the Mediterranean, the Aegean, and the Baltic had once served Europe. They turned a united nation into one nation.

The railroaders knew the economic meaning of government and they expected the government to do their bidding. As early as 1843, James Buchanan noted their irresistible influence: "If you defeat them at this session they will be here in greater force than ever at the commencement of the next. Their importunity will never cease whilst the least hope of success shall remain, and we have learned from our

6 John M. Blum et al., *The National Experience* (New York: Harcourt, Brace & World, 1968), p. 437.
7 Thomas C. Cochran and William Miller, *The Age of Enterprise* (New York: Harper & Row, 1961), pp. 67–68.

experience that they have both the ability and the will to select shrewd and skillful agents to accomplish their purposes before Congress."

These skillful agents had a whole arsenal full of persuasive goodies for legislators—railroad stock, investment tips, free passes. Among the "prominent participants in railroad favors were Senators Stephen A. Douglas, Lewis Cass, and Thomas Benton, each an investor in western lands, a speculator in railroad securities. Between 1850 and 1870, they helped the railroads to 25,000 acres of public land, free beyond the cost of their own unofficial services. From willing states and cities lesser politicians got enormous railroad loans."[8] They even got Congress to lower the tariff on British rails.

After the Civil War, the railroads really began to roll. In the postbellum decade, mileage was doubled—from 35,000 to 70,000. By the end of the century, the U.S. had more mileage than all of Europe, including Russia—a total of 200,000 miles. Government supplied the land and much of the capital. Congress gave away 131,000,000 acres of land plus tens of millions of dollars in loans. States offered $228 million in bonds and the like. Even the counties, cities, towns, and villages contributed some $300 million.

The land grants to the railroads gave them more than the narrow terrain on which to lay rails. The Pacific Railway Act of 1862, for instance, gave the road five square miles on each side of the track. These tracts were laid out in checkerboard fashion, alternating railroad and government property. By law, these parcels of government land were withheld from homesteaders, thereby tending to weaken the Homestead Act that was passed the same year. Senator Howe of Wisconsin complained that the railroad grants were making "the whole Northwest and the whole West but little more than a province of New York."

By other acts—legislative and executive—the original policy of distributing public lands to the little people was reversed to benefit the land engrossers: railroads, mining

[8] Ibid., p. 78.

and lumber companies, real-estate speculators. The Homestead Act itself was warped by unchecked corruption. Speculators "hired men to stake out claims, falsely swear that they had fulfilled the conditions laid down in the law for obtaining legal title, and then deed the land over to their employers."[9]

Because much of the western land was unsuitable for small-scale farming, the federal government decided to allow a grant of an additional 160 acres to homesteaders under the Timber Culture Act of 1873. But that well-intentioned piece of legislation suffered the same sad fate as the Homestead Act. "The government permitted private interests to gobble up and destroy many of the great forests that clothed the slopes of the Rockies and the Sierras."[10]

The Timber and Stone Act of 1878 allowed a man to buy up forest land for $2.50 an acre if it was "unfit for civilization." Again, the corporations moved in, sending in long lines of dummies to buy up property. "In many instances whole townships have been entered under this law in the interest of one person or firm, to whom the lands have been conveyed as soon as receipts for the purchase price were issued," reported the commissioner of the General Land Office in 1901.

In 1876, Congress took almost 50 million acres of southern land that had been reserved for homesteaders and threw it onto the open market. The speculators swarmed in.

The Morrill Act granted federal land to states to encourage colleges for instruction "in agriculture and mechanical arts." Since the eastern states did not have such land, the federal government gave them scrip for 7,500,000 acres of land in the West that could be sold to raise funds for eastern colleges. The scrip swiftly became a negotiable item used by speculators for quick gain. "With Agricultural College scrip of New York, Ezra Cornell located nearly 500,000 acres in Wisconsin, Minnesota and Kansas. . . .

[9] John A. Garraty, *The American Nation* (New York: Harper & Row, 1966), p. 487.
[10] Ibid., p. 488.

Amos Lawrence, Boston Associate, promoter, with others of the Emigrant Aid Company, located 58,360 acres in Kansas in 1866 with Agricultural College scrip, while the Emigrant Aid Company itself, through transactions not always legitimate, purchased 800,000 acres of Cherokee lands at a dollar an acre."[11]

"Through its land program," concluded historian Louis Hacker, "the Republican Party laid the foundation for some great land, timber and mineral fortunes."[12]

Policies on taxes and tariffs—like those on land and finance—served corporate interests. And so did labor policy. When employers complained about a labor shortage during the war years, Congress enacted a Contract Labor Law that validated contracts signed overseas and exempted such imported labor from military service. Instantly, employers pooled funds to form the American Emigrant Company to recruit cheap labor around the world. The employee had to pledge his first year's pay to cover the expenses of his transportation to America.

"Industrial capitalism was in that idyllic state where it could have its cake and eat it. The government gave it a protected market, a railroad net, a cheap labor supply, a sound currency—and shunted the costs onto the backs of workers and farmers."[13]

As William Allen White viewed the Congress in 1889, the legislature was a collage of business interests. "A United States senator . . . represented something more than a state, more even than a region. One senator, for instance, represented the Union Pacific Railway System, another the New York Central, still another the insurance interests of New York and New Jersey. Coal and iron owned a coterie from the Middle and Eastern seaport states. Cotton had a half dozen senators. And so it went."[14]

[11] Cochran and Miller, *Age of Enterprise,* p. 109.
[12] Louis Hacker, *The Triumph of American Capitalism* (New York: Simon and Schuster, 1940), p. 371.
[13] Ibid., p. 363.
[14] William Allen White, *Masks in a Pageant* (New York: Macmillan Company, 1928), p. 79.

By the turn of the century, the *Bankers' Magazine* foresaw a nation run both politically and economically by the capitalist. "As the business of the country has learned the secret of combination," they wrote in 1901, "it is gradually subverting the power of the politician and rendering him subservient to its purposes. . . . That [government is not] entirely controlled by these interests is due to the fact that business organization has not reached full perfection."[15]

In the next three decades, business learned to perfect its political controls. It also learned the great secret of all true performers, the *ars celare artem*—the art of concealing the art. Business learned to elect dummies who looked independent and couched their appeals in the language of the people.

Business also learned how to hide its dependence on and use of governmental power by loudly announcing its belief in laissez faire. In possession of the nation's economy and in control of its political apparatus, business denounced all state interference in the nation's business.

The unsuspecting, including a large number of intellectuals, really believed that laissez faire was the businessman's deeply felt ideology. It never was. Businessmen opposed state intervention when such public action got in the way of what the businessmen wanted to do. Otherwise, they favored laws, executive actions, court interpretations, police behavior that served their own interests—or crushed any opposition from business competitors, labor, or the consumer.

The "robber barons" who dominated the American scene during the Age of Enterprise—from the Civil War to the New Deal—"had no ideology; they had interests. . . . This elite lived at the public trough, was nourished by state protection and devoted most of its time and energies to evading Adam Smith's individualistic injunctions. In ideological terms it was totally opportunist," notes historian and political scientist John Roche. "It demanded and applauded vigorous state action in behalf of its key values,

[15] *Bankers' Magazine*, Vol. LXII, 1901, p. 498.

and denounced state intervention in behalf of its enemies."[16]

To business, laissez faire simply meant, Let us do unto others as we please but do not let others do unto us. And in this game without rules, let us name the umpire.

[16] John Roche, *Sentenced to Life* (New York: Macmillan Company, 1974), p. 205.

3

The Return of Abundance

The New Deal was not the beginning of governmental intervention into the world of business. From the settlement of the colonies in 1609 to the unsettlement of the economy in 1929, government—especially the federal government—was uninterruptedly involved in the monied affairs of the so-called private sector.

The New Deal differed from previous uses of such power in two respects. First, the Rooseveltians frankly admitted that they were out to use the levers of federal power to lift the economy out of the slump and to put it on the road to recovery. They abandoned the hypocrisy of laissez faire. Second, the New Deal added a few representatives of the toiling classes to the "state" that was, until then, a fairly undiluted "executive committee of the ruling class."

Neither of these objectives was a purpose proclaimed by Roosevelt in the election of 1932. To combat the Depression, he proposed "less"—not more—government, in the traditional rhetoric of the Jeffersonians. Specifically, he campaigned on a program to cut federal spending.

The New Deal evolved out of groping responses to an absurdity: palpable poverty amidst potential plenty. We had plenty of capital, especially if "capital" is counted as productive plant: factories were idle and machinery was rusting. We had plenty of resources and raw material. We had managerial know-how and an educated and eager labor force. We had people hungry for things. We had everything needed for prosperity—everything except a market.

Without a market, the producer does not produce. In the lore of laissez faire, it is the market that summons the entrepreneur into action, telling him what to manufacture and in what quantity and quality. The producer hearkens to the market. But if the market is silent, then the producer is still.

One of the unnoted contradictions of capitalism is the total dependence of the producer on a strong market and the total unwillingness of the same producer to strengthen the market—if it costs him anything. As a seller, each capitalist would like to see masses with money buying up his wares. As an employer, the same capitalist sees increased earnings by his employees as a cost. Schizophrenically, then, he insists on greater buying power and resists employee demands that would expand such buying power.

Because the entrepreneurial class was paralyzed by the innate strife between its hopes as seller and its fears as employer, the New Deal had to bypass voluntarism in the private sector to enact compulsory measures for recovery. Such measures were variations on a simple single theme: expand aggregate demand.

To "prime the pump," it was necessary to take money from where it was and put it where it wasn't. The federal government used its taxing and borrowing powers to direct spending money to those most likely to spend it: namely, the unemployed.

The numerous programs that the government set up— WPA, PWA, FERA, CCC, CWA, NYA—were irksome to the American spirit. The "alphabet soup" was denounced as a distasteful, debilitating diet. It was shameless and shameful "made-work," paying people for doing nothing, a hand out, a dole.

Since the early New Deal days, a mean little debate has raged around the subject of whether these "projects" were worthwhile. Defenders of the "works" tried to prove that monies appropriated went to build libraries, replenish forests, paint works of art, survey slums for clearance and rehabilitation. Critics pointed to cases where one gang swept fallen leaves from here to there to be followed by another gang to sweep the leaves from there to here.

Both sides could prove their point. And both points were irrelevant. The object of the pump-priming projects was not to rebuild America but to recover the economy. The "works" were a way of putting people to work, not necessarily to create anything more than more buying power.

In this spirit, other measures followed, such as the Fair Labor Standards Act, commonly referred to as the minimum-wage law. This piece of legislation did not put jobless on the job. It simply sought to raise the income of people already on the job who, because of their low pay, might just as well have had no jobs—in terms of their buying power. Three dollars a week for a sixty-hour week at five cents an hour added little to "aggregate demand." The new law set a floor of twenty-five cents an hour for wages and a ceiling of forty hours of work a week.

In industries paying five cents an hour, employers protested despairingly that this four hundred percent increase in wages would have to bankrupt them. But it didn't, because with a small increase in selling prices and a massive expansion of the market, they were able to make ends meet and, indeed, to profit as they never had before.

Since most workers were not unemployed (only between one-quarter and one-third were) and since most workers made more than twenty-five cents an hour, the next item on the New Deal agenda was to raise the wages—increase the buying power—of those men and women who had jobs and were making more than the federal legal minimum. A first step was to call together representatives of employers and of employees to agree on some industry-wide basis for wages. The companies that complied would be allowed to make a proud display of the Blue Eagle, the symbol of the NRA (National Recovery Act).

This venture quickly revealed that while employers generally had associations to speak for them, very few workers had organizations—unions—to speak for them. Hence, a vital element in a national recovery program was the encouragement of a labor voice. Such an instrumentality was embodied in Section 7a of the NRA—encouraging workers to join unions of their own choosing and hailing collective bargaining as a public good.

Both unions and purchasing power rose meteorically. Whereas unions spoke for about 5 percent of the labor force in the early thirties, they represented more than 35 percent a decade later. Personal-consumption expenditures rose from a lowly $45 billion in 1933 to $99 billion in 1943. In constant dollars (1958 dollars) that was a rise from $112 billion to $165 billion. Buying power in real dollars grew by almost 50 percent in a decade.

Section 7a moved new ethnic, as well as economic, elements into the dynamic for expanding demand. Prior to the union surge of the thirties and forties, the unionized sectors of the economy were among the "aristocrats" of labor in the building and construction trades, railroading, the graphics (printing), and machinists, pattern-makers, molders, and other skilled crafts in manufacturing. These people were, by and large, the settled stock of the working class: English-speaking, early immigrant, white. The post-7a generation was made up heavily of the semi- and unskilled in mass manufacture: steel, auto, rubber, textile, apparel, electronics. These were, much more than the people in the skilled crafts, of recent immigrant stock, blacks from the plantations of the South, whites from the hills of Appalachia, and hispanics out of the Southwest. When mass manufacture was unionized, these new elements became union members. The movement of these racial and ethnic elements into the economic dynamic meant that great new layers of the nation would be pushing on their own for their version of rights and riches. While the New Deal concept of expanding aggregate demand began as a "revolution" from above, the notion was easily and instinctively accepted by those once economically disfranchised to become a revolution from below.

While unions helped boost the earnings (buying power) of those at work, they were able to do very little for those who were out of work because of a business slack, a bankruptcy, or old age. To do something to maintain a modicum of buying power for workers caught in these hazards, the New Deal provided special "incomes" during bad times. For those temporarily out of work, there was unemployment compensation—some income during periods of involuntary idleness. For those "too old to work but too young to die" there was social security—a source of spending money as well as solace for the aged.

In subsequent decades, the central idea of maximizing employment by maximizing purchasing power became the hidden agenda behind public housing, federal aid to education, nationally financed health care, the Tennessee Valley Authority, a national highway program. Each of these projects had its own reason for being—a home for the homeless, schooling for future citizens, hospitals for the sick, electricity for rural America, an avenue for transport or travel. These were all humane and sensible investments that allowed government to rush in where the financial angels of the private sector feared to tread. But beyond and behind the proclaimed rationale was the secret reason—more work, stimulated by governmental demand.

The recovery was slow, dragging over nearly a decade. The pre-Depression level was not regained until 1939, when the United States became the arsenal of democracy. This timing has prompted the conclusion that it was not the New Deal but the war followed by wars, from 1939 on, that pulled the nation out of its deep depression. This thesis is particularly popular among the latter-day opponents of the Rooseveltian schema who resist the idea of expanded buying power as the stimulant for economic activity.

The ups and downs of our gross national income (or gross national product) between the years 1929 and 1939, however, make it perfectly plain that America was well on the road to recovery prior to the outbreak of the Second World War. Start with 1929, which was the best and worst year of its decade—the best because output was at a record high, with total national income standing at $84.7 billion, 6.6 percent above 1928; the worst because at the end of 1929 came the beginning of the Great Depression with its sagging income. In constant dollars (1958 dollars) income fell from $161 billion in 1929, to $146 billion in 1930, to $131 billion in 1931, to $110 billion in 1932, to $107 billion in 1933. And then, in 1934—the year after Roosevelt took office—the national income (still in constant 1958 dollars) began to rise to $119 billion, in 1935 to $134 billion, in 1936 to $152 billion, in 1937 to $163 billion (back to the 1929 record high), and then in 1939 to $165 billion.[1]

As we entered the era of permanent warfare—from 1939 on—the national income turned an upward climb into an upward flight. In 1942, the first year of America's direct participation in World War II, national income (constant dollars) rose to $249 billion—a 45-percent leap over 1939. By 1944, the sum had risen to $304 billion—an 80-percent rise over 1939. The economy was soaring.

Expenditures for national defense were a major, although never the sole, factor in lifting the national income to these heights. In 1939, before entering active combat, we spent a meaningless $1.2 billion on national defense. That was about 2 percent as big as the sum spent in personal consumption ($66 billion). But by 1942, we spent almost $50 billion on national defense, a sum more than half the amount spent on total personal consumption ($88.5 billion). And in 1944, we spent more than $87 billion on national defense, a sum that was about 80 percent of what was spent on personal consumption ($108 billion).[2]

While military expenditures then added fresh fuel to our economic engine, they were by no means the sole source of our productive energy, as is obvious from the rising amounts for personal consumption during the war years. Even more revealing, however, are the figures for the post–World War II years when the nation became involved in lesser conflicts. Expenditures on national defense fell, but personal consumption continued to expand and to spur economic growth.

[1] Edward F. Denison, *Accounting for United States Economic Growth, 1929–1969* (Washington, D.C.: The Brookings Institution, 1974), p. 163.
[2] *Handbook of Labor Statistics, 1974*, U.S. Department of Labor, p. 249.

By 1947, for instance, an early postwar year, expenditures on national defense fell to $9.1 billion, which was less than 6 percent of what was spent on personal consumption and less than 4 percent of the Gross National Product. Even at the height of the Vietnam war, the total spent on military expenditures was only 12 percent of the sum spent on personal consumption and only 9 percent of the GNP.[3]

The years of relatively full employment, from 1939 to 1969, were not dependent on military expenditures for jobs. The propaganda of the right that wished to discredit the New Deal and the agitation of the left that wished to depict America as a "war economy" merged to spread the impression that American prosperity depended on a state of war. Actually, the true basis for economic expansion was expanded buying power in the private—not the military—sector.

But even if military expenditures were responsible for economic expansion, such an unpleasant finding would not contradict the fact that the driving motor of the economic machine was expanded aggregate demand. The demand for military purposes—men, munitions, and ammunitions—is just one aspect of aggregate demand. And—as humanitarian critics of the American regime are always ready to point out—the same great sums spent on planes, battleships, and MIRV missiles could be spent on child care, hospitals, cancer research, and the feeding of the hungry. In either event, whether the federal funds are used to end someone's life or to restore someone else's life, the expenditure out of the governmental coffers goes toward expanding aggregate demand—the basis for a fuller employment economy.

To friend and foe alike, the new Rooseveltian system was known as "the welfare state." To its advocates, this meant a government devoted to the fulfillment of the promise contained in the preamble of the Constitution of the United States: to "promote the general welfare." To its critics, this meant a government that was about to put the whole country on "welfare," to treat the citizenry as a charity case. Both sides agreed that the government, especially the

[3] Ibid., p. 250.

federal government, was spending inordinate and ever-larger sums of public funds to maintain welfarism. Friends thought this was good; foes thought it was bad. But both seemed to agree on the facts.

Yet again, as in the myth that the society was dependent on huge military budgets to maintain a viable economy, the impression that the government, especially the federal government, has been financing an ever-larger portion of the economy turns out to be fantasy, unfounded in fact.

The illusion that the federal government was buying up the economy—"creeping socialism"—found a modicum of validity in the World War II era. In one such typical year, 1943, the government—federal, state, and local—spent a sum equal to that spent for all personal consumption: public expenditure was almost half the Gross National Product. And the federal government was responsible for about 90 percent of all public purchases.

But in the postwar years, governmental expenditures fell to levels of 10 to 20 percent of the GNP. And in the post–Korean War years, the federal share of the expenditures fell as compared with the expenditures of state and local governments. In the five-year period from 1946 to 1950, total government expenditures—federal, state, and local—ran at an average of a mere 12.6 percent of the GNP: 13 percent in 1946, 10.7 in 1947, 12 in 1948, 14.7 in 1949, 13 in 1950.[4] The purely *federal* share of the expenditures ran to about half the amount—averaging between 6 and 7 percent of the GNP, a striking irony since these were the years of President Harry S. Truman with his Democratic dedication to the Fair Deal, touted as an expansion of the New Deal.

Government spending—as a percentage of GNP—did not show any significant rise until the Korean War buildup in 1951. But even then, the rise was negligible—from 13 percent in 1950 to 18 percent in 1951. And from that year on, government spending has remained an amazingly steady percentage of the GNP at about 21 percent—with a low of 18 in 1951 and a high of 22.6 in 1967.[5]

[4] Ibid., p. 249.
[5] Ibid.

For almost a full generation, then—from 1951 to 1975—one dollar out of every five in the GNP was spent by government. The formula seems fixed, no matter what party sits in the White House.

During these years, the federal portion of governmental spending has been shrinking from 70 percent of public expenditures in 1953 to 38 percent in 1973. The drop appears "nonpolitical," since the decline is fairly steady and continues its downward course through both Democratic and Republican administrations. From the high 70 percent in 1953, the federal percentage slid to 57 in 1958, to 52 in 1963, to 49.4 in 1968 (the Vietnam apex), and to 38 in 1973. Simultaneously, of course, state and local percentages varied inversely—rising from 30 percent to 62 percent.[6]

Taken in toto, then, the experiences after World War II suggested that the United States could experience "prosperity" without either "war" or "socialism." All the key words in quotes are, of course, to be read with relative meaning. To wit:

• Government expenditures that equal one-fifth of the GNP—with federal spending at less than half of that—hardly make America a "socialist" society. (In 1973, gross domestic investments were double federal expenditures, and personal consumption was almost eight times as great.) Nevertheless, the role of the government in the economy has been considerably enlarged in the years since 1929, when total government spending was only 8 percent of the GNP and federal spending only 1 percent.

• Likewise, the American economy can hardly be defined as a "war economy" in the years after World War II: expenditures on national defense over all the years from 1947 to 1973 averaged about 8 percent of the GNP—starting with a low of 4 percent in 1947, rising to a high of 13 percent in 1952 and 1953, during Korea, then declining to a 9-percent level during Vietnam, and falling to less than 6 percent in 1973. And yet, there is no doubt that the lesser

[6] Ibid.

wars did add to the aggregate demand that stimulated economic growth.

• Finally, the term "prosperity" must be taken with a grain of salt. The average unemployment rate in the years from 1947 to 1973 ran at 4.7 percent, which is hardly *full* employment. Nevertheless, at no time in those years did the level even reach 7 percent and, at no time did the dips in the economy along the way turn into anything even distantly resembling the Great Depression.[7]

The American assumption of abundance seemed to have been revalidated. The United States had somehow found a way to keep the ship of state on an even keel and to move its passengers on to ever more pleasant climes. The national income kept growing uninterruptedly. In constant dollars, the GNP moved from $203 billion in 1929 to $209 billion in 1939, to $324 billion in 1949, to $475 billion in 1959, to $725 billion in 1969, to $837 billion in 1973.[8] To the man in the street, however, an even more significant and personal statistic was per capita income, since he was one of the counted capita. Here, if 1958 is used as the index year (100), then per capita income rose from 65.80 in 1940 to 141.77 in 1969, more than doubling real income in a little more than one generation.[9]

Even the occasional dips along the way turned out to be reassuring as the ship of state rose high on the next crest. The most challenging of these experiences came after World War II when the economy fell into a trough: the all-time high GNP of $361 billion (1958 dollars) in 1944 dipped to $355 billion the next year, then fell to $309 billion in 1947 —a 20-percent decline in three years. Things looked bad.[10]

The threatening look of things came as no surprise to those seers who had been predicting postwar economic disaster. During the war years, the nation's productive system had undergone a technological revolution in the effort to

[7] Ibid., p. 27.
[8] Ibid., p. 250.
[9] Denison, *Economic Growth, 1929–1969*, p. 13.
[10] *Handbook of Labor Statistics, 1974*, p. 250.

produce enough to meet both civilian and military demand. Machines were invented that had eyes, ears, and brains as well as muscles. Automation and computerization and cybernation were, it seemed, rendering human workers obsolete. What then would we do when some twelve million men and women in uniform returned to civilian life at a time when the demand for military wares would fall off? The obvious forecast was for another major depression.

That depression never came because of a postwar demand for goods and services that was great enough to absorb the prodigious output of an automated economy. That demand came from several sources:

• Workers in mass manufacture increased their hourly wage. They had been in the habit of working overtime during the war years and to earn the extra pay of the extra hours at extra rates. When the war ended, they demanded the same weekly pay for a regular work week. In this objective, they were more or less successful—thereby maintaining their buying power despite reduced work hours. In 1944, a war year, production workers in manufacture were making $46.08 a week in a 45.2-hour work week. By 1947, they were making $49.97 a week for a 40.4-hour work week. Loss of overtime pay did not reduce weekly earnings.[11]

• During the war, the nation was on a regimen of forced savings—war bonds purchased out of paychecks. When the war ended, these bonds were converted into cash and buying power.

• During the war, unions held back on wage demands because they were considered inflationary. Instead, contracts called for deferred "wage" payments in the form of retirement pay, health programs, optical and maternity care, etc. When the war ended, these labor-management fringe benefits matured—adding to the demand for goods and services.

• By war's end, the welfare-state program of the New Deal had matured. Millions of people were on retirement

[11] *Historical Statistics of the United States, Colonial Times to 1957,* U.S. Bureau of the Census, 1960, p. 92.

or on programs of aid for the blind, handicapped, or otherwise dependent—like children in a home without a breadwinner. These "welfare" payments added to buying power.

• Returnees from the war married, gave birth to children, bought homes, cars, and utensils—often confidently on the installment plan. This added to aggregate demand.

• The federal government expressed its thanks in cash to the servicemen and women who had saved the nation. A GI bill gave scholarships plus living expenses to millions of veterans; it also made easy loans for the purchase of homes or to set up a business. This open-handed generosity added to aggregate demand.

• The United States created customers overseas. By cash and credit to the bleeding and backward nations of the earth, the United States stimulated an overseas market.

For all these reasons, expanded demand was able to absorb the expanded output of the automated economy.

While very few Americans had any idea at all of what was happening, almost everybody had the feeling that if the United States was able to sail securely through the stormy waters of the postwar period, then this nation could go ahead, with confidence that there would be an abundant America to the end of time.

The economy expanded far beyond the expectations of almost everyone, including the utopians. When Vice-President Henry Wallace was warming up for his maverick, quixotic campaign as the Progressive Party candidate for President of the United States, he called for radical reforms that would make us a nation with "Sixty Million Jobs." The dreamy slogan was coined in 1945, when there were 53 million in the civilian labor force and an additional twelve million in the military. Just two years later—1947—the civilian labor force had expanded to more than 60 million and then just kept growing right down to 1975, when the civilian labor force was above 90 million.

Nor was this increase purely due to an increase in the population: the civilian labor force was growing more rapidly than the population. In 1945, the percentage of the population (over age 14) in the labor force was 50; by 1947, it was 55.8; by 1973, it was close to 60.

The economic euphoria reached into the American household as family income climbed. In 1947, the median income was $3,301 for the year. That income zoomed up to $10,285 by 1971.

America had rediscovered abundance—a traditional plenitude that promised to go on forever.

4

The Iron Law of Maldistribution

In the economic theology of America, Growth was God. So long as It was in Its Heaven, all was well on earth. Everybody could live better—poor as well as rich. The blessings of this man-made deity, like manna from above, could rain down on all.

In the dazzling brilliance of this luminous Almighty, the nation was blinded to an ugly flaw in the body politic: a dangerous maldistribution of our national income. This weakness in our societal character—like most Achilles' heels —was not easy to find.

The popular impression was that past inequities were being slowly righted, that national income was being redistributed toward the middle. The poor were no longer so poor; the rich no longer so rich. Everybody was being reclassified into the middle class—upper, lower, or middle middle.

Those who were in the "middle class" came to this conclusion through personal experience. The average white family saw its income rise from $5,714 in 1947 to $10,672 in 1971. The average black family saw its income rise from $2,930 to $6,714 in the same time. Both increases were in real dollars, adjusted for changes in prices. In a decade and a half, the average white family had doubled its true income and the average black family had more than doubled its income.[1]

Millions of these middle-class Americans had come up from the ranks of the poor—that is, the officially poor. In 1959, there were 39.5 million persons officially listed as living below poverty level; by 1971, that number was reduced to 25.6 million. The percentage of people living in poverty was just about cut in two, from 22 to 12 percent.

While the remaining "poor" were not personally going through this metamorphosis, they saw enough of their kindred pass into the new life to give the feeling that ultimately the transfiguration could—would—come to all.

The rich—as usual—were not talking about their net worth nor were they encouraging anyone else to talk about it. If they spoke at all, it was through the mouths of corporations crying over low profits.

Official statistics did not correct the misimpression. Indeed, they added to the broadly accepted, but totally false, image.

If one consulted the official report on *Consumer Income* (December 1973) issued by the U.S. Department of Commerce, it appeared that family income was being effectively redistributed—albeit at a snail's pace. Thus in 1947, the aggregate income of the bottom fifth of the nation was a miserable 5.1 percent of the total national income. But by 1972, that share of the national income had risen to 5.4 percent. While that change is hardly revolutionary—three-tenths of one percent in a quarter-century—it is a change of some sort that, if continued, could gain the bottom 20 percent of the families 7 percent of the national income if they had the patience to sweat it out over a century.

Meanwhile, the top fifth was giving way on its share of the national income—from 43.3 percent in 1947 to 41.4 percent in 1968, a loss of 1.9 percent in twenty-five years.

Even the top 5 percent of the families—the untouchables of the economic order—were suffering losses from their take

[1] *Statistical Abstract of the United States, 1973,* U.S. Bureau of the Census, p. 329.

of 17.5 percent of the income in 1947 to 15.9 percent in 1968—a slippage of 1.6 percent.[2]

The table confirmed the tune of the times: we're all going down the middle.

But the table was totally misleading—because of the way in which it defined "income." The Department of Commerce, in making its calculations, excludes certain types of income —namely, "money received from the sale of property, such as stocks, bonds, a house, or a car . . . gifts . . . and lump sum inheritances or insurance payments."

These excluded incomes are all the kind of incomes one is likely to find bulking large in the true—not the official— incomes of the rich, especially the top 5 or—better—the top one percent. If we include these forms of income, then the total income of the nation rises, the share of the rich rises, and just about everybody else's share falls.

The size of these unreported incomes is much greater than one may unsuspectingly expect. Consider the year of 1968, for instance:

The incomes officially reported to the Census Bureau that year totaled $543 billion. But there was an additional $76 billion in cash income that was not reported; an additional $18 billion in capital gains; an additional $27 billion in undistributed profits; and an additional $76 billion in "imputed income," like the imputed rent that goes to the owner-occupier of a house as the building gains in equity value. A grand sum of $188 billion dollars of income—equal to a third of the reported income—goes uncounted in the official reports on income distribution. The inclusion of the excluded monies turns the tables topsy-turvy.[3]

If we zero in on just one item of that nonincluded income—capital gains—we find that the percentage of the national income derived from this source has been rising from 1.6 percent to 2.9 percent in the years from 1954 to 1967. Since capital gains are a rich man's source of income,

[2] *"Consumer Income," Current Population Reports,* 1973, U.S. Bureau of the Census, p. 45.
[3] Roger A. Herriot and Herman P. Miller, "The Taxes We Pay," *The Conference Board Record,* VIII (May 1971).

the increase in this income factor necessarily increases the rich man's share of the national income.

Not surprisingly, such capital gains make up an ever increasing portion of true income for the rich. Those with an income of more than $100,000 a year derived 22 percent of their income from capital gains in 1954, 23 percent in 1956, and 29 percent in 1967. But these gains were not included in the officially calculated incomes of the top 5 percent.[4]

Those with an income of more than $100,000 showed an ever increasing share of their receipts derived from capital gains.

CAPITAL GAINS IN INDIVIDUAL INCOME TAX
(BILLIONS OF $)

	1954	1956	1967
Adjusted Gross Income	$229.2	$267.7	$504.8
Net Capital Gains[5]	$ 3.7	$ 5.0	$ 14.4
Capital Gains % of AGI	1.6%	1.9%	2.9%
Capital Gains to Those of AGI Over $100,000	$ .813	$ 1.15	$ 4.2
% of Capital Gains to Those of AGI Over $100,000	22 %	23 %	29 %

Quite obviously, the Commerce figures showing the top 5 percent with 14 percent of the income in 1968 is a patent understatement of their share of the income. Consequently, too, the 5.7 percent of the income credited to the lowest fifth is an overstatement. Plainly, the rich get a much bigger bite than the government tables reveal and the poor get a much smaller bite.

An accurate portrayal of how national income is distributed would include earnings from capital gains, real estate sales, gifts, inheritances, etc. Once these "hidden"

---

[4] The figures on income from capital gains are derived from data furnished by the Internal Revenue Service and have been analyzed, as sketched above, by Arnold Kantor, staff economist of the AFL-CIO.
[5] Net capital gains *reported* in AGI—does not include the *excluded* half of gains. Therefore actual gains are roughly double figures shown. Also does not include capital gains passed on at death.

incomes are brought to light, the true distribution—maldistribution—of income becomes shockingly clear.

In a rare and masterful piece of research and reasoning, two imaginative economists who were attached to the Bureau of Census, Herman P. Miller and Roger A. Herriot, recomputed income distribution by converting the excluded incomes into included incomes. Their findings showed the great gap between what the Commerce Department said was so and what is really so. For instance:

By the way the Commerce Department calculated income, a small group of consumer units with incomes above $50,000—actually less than one-half of one percent of all consumer units—received 2 percent of the total income in 1968. But, if one includes the missing income that the Commerce Department deigns not to count, then the same tiny group of consumer units picks up 7 percent of the national income annually.

By official count, 2 percent of the families earning over $25,000 a year in 1968 got 9 percent of the income. But if the missing income is included, the same 2 percent earned 18 percent of the total.

To get some idea as to how dangerously lopsidedly income is distributed, contrast the earnings of the top 2.5 percent with the bottom 27 percent (earning less than $4,000 a year in 1968). The top 2.5 percent picks up 18 percent of the national income—which is four and a half times as much as is earned by the bottom 27 percent, who get only 4 percent of the income.[6] By the same count, a top 1.4 percent had an income equal to the bottom 34 percent.[7]

Calculations done by others than Herriot and Miller do not necessarily reach exactly the same conclusions. In 1970, a team of young Harvard researchers tried to figure out what the distribution would be if receipts on capital gains were included as "income." Digging into the year 1962, they con-

[6] Roger A. Herriot and Herman P. Miller, "Tax Changes Among Income Groups, 1962–1968," *Business Horizons*, February 1972.
[7] Roger A. Herriot and Herman P. Miller, "Who Paid the Taxes in 1968" (Paper prepared for the National Industrial Conference Board, March 18, 1971).

cluded that the top one percent received an income almost equal to the bottom 40 percent.[8]

While this finding differs from the Herriot-Miller finding for 1968, the difference is negligible. Whether it is one or 2 percent at the top with an income equal to either the 34 or 40 percent at the bottom is a matter of minutiae alongside the gross inequities revealed in every dig into the way our goods and services are divvied up. Statisticians quibble about a few points here or there, but there is no argument about the real point on income maldistribution.

Theoretically, the American tax system is supposed to rectify some of these inequities. According to legend, the rich may make more, much more, but after the bigwigs pay their heavy taxes, the extremes between the top and bottom are not quite as extreme as they seem to be. In other words, after-tax incomes are much closer together than before-tax incomes.

Taxes, however, fail to restore income equity. Many at the top pay virtually no federal income tax because of special loopholes. In the states where the income tax is based on the federal tax, the same individuals avoid their state tax in the same way and in the same degree.

But even among those who do not escape their responsibility through loopholes, there is very little progressivity in the tax—if one includes federal, state, and local levies. Thus, in 1968, those making less than $2,000 a year paid a total tax equal to 26 percent of their income and those making between $25,000 and $50,000 a year paid 33 percent of their income. Those earning in between paid in-between percentages. The difference in the rate of payment between those earning the bottom $2,000 and those earning the much higher $50,000 was negligible.[9]

Consequently, the inequities of maldistribution before taxes are not substantially corrected after taxes.

The maldistribution of income is reflected in the maldistribution of wealth. The difference between "income" and

[8] Gus Tyler, "The White Worker" (Unpublished paper prepared for the American Jewish Committee).
[9] Herriot and Miller, "Tax Changes, 1962–1968."